Need I Say 'More'

AyPress

Ann Marie Yeager

AyPress
3546 Steubenville Rd., SE
Amsterdam, OH 43903

AyPress and its colophon ("lions guarding
sun") are trademarks of AyPress.

Published and Printed in the United States
of America.

AyPress website: www.aypress.com

Library of Congress Catalogue-in-Publication
Data: Yeager, Ann Marie, 1966-;
1. Philosophy I. Title II. Author
2003093963

First Edition, Hardcover

ISBN: 0-9742582-3-7

1 11 22 33 44 55 66 77 88 99

Distributed to the trade by Ingram

"There is one (thing) I wish to see
in moral philosophy,
the discovery of a plan,
that would induce and oblige nations
to settle their disputes
without first cutting one another's throats..."

-Franklin

It is not for the lack of the plan,
but the lack of the brave will
to be vulnerable
while the plan executes and adheres itself
to the realities of even the most pessimistic.

To balance an object is difficult.
There is only one perfect spot on its axis;
achieved by the growth of opposites.

To begin to be the instrument,
you must believe in the magnitude
of your ability.

We learn the same thing over, many times,
when we do not learn.
The teacher (adjective) is always disguised.

A secret—is a lie.

People who complain, n'er think.
E'er on the brink—of war of stink.

A planet (not created by man),
is taxed to live on (by man),
for man's belief.

A mite—brings down
the mightiest oak.
Does the oak—fear to grow?

If the secret is in the sauce—
what need is there for cloning?
Man uses animal, to test his ambitions on man.

Is there free will,
when men do not think,
but merely side with arguments and adjectives?

Hero—is an adjective to describe
a societal state of decay.

If there is no equality in debate—
there is no justice in enactment.

(Lie detector test, etc.)

When people accept machinery—
in place of humans—
they will no longer accept humans.

(Importance of directions in Feng Shui.)

Someone's west—is another's north.

One does not determine the answer.

The answer is determined.

To determine the answer—brings chaos.

Any member of an elected office,
who vacates said office during any session,
silences the voices of his constituents.

Murder—may value life;
but suicide—values the soul.
Death is individual.
But its legacy—inaugural.

What determines if one's "bad" or "good,"
isn't if one would help one's friends—
but if one would harm one's enemies.

When feeling anger—
and believe destruction is solution—
do nothing.

The feeling will pass.
The action will remain.
The path—is the teacher.

Those who argue:
"It's my house"; *"I pay the bills"*;
believe:
a just government—is a dictatorship.

Men worry about being bankrupt—
while they bankrupt men's souls.

Bequeathed a thousand pairs of used shoes
is the greatest gift of sight.

Educational institutions,
who condone student drinking—
do not respect the mind*,
but the wallet.

(*Erosion of brain.)

Criminal act in prison—
consents approval of crime.

Men who appreciate only "breasts,"
have "malnourished" souls.

Freedom—
is not what imposes its will
upon any other;
nor is it being enraptured
in others' thoughts.

It is easy to be polite—in comfort.
Comfort's acclimation—
lay in mind.

Religions' moral?
Perfection—can only be obtained—
through another's death.

Religion's psychology divides men,
to know who is willing to believe anything,
and who is not;
so men may rule—at will—
without question or interference?

Dream—is contained to "self";
hence, its last "suffix": "am."

People confuse "dream" and "will."
Will—afflicts dream.

Everything is dust.
It is only made tangible—
by dreams.

Writing too many lines:
unfeeling.
Do not know when to stop.

A photo may inspire a thousand words.
But—its every word—assumes.

Heat has the power to turn.
We revolve—by the heat of the sun.

'Tis better to die in (teaching) trust—
than live in fear.
Trust—is the equability of progress.

Fear—is a tool for profit.
Man has made money—more powerful—
than God.

Suit perceived.
Apparel—is "apparent apprehension."
Genius—shines from words.

Men take off shirts—
to divert attention from the eyes.

If man desires a higher position in life,
he thinks to improve his trade of labor;
not the totality of his mind.

Legs crossed: logical thinker.
Legs apart: emotional thinker.

/ -   - /
An objected house—is an objected mind:
concerned with retaining—not producing.

There is redundancy in the word "committee,"
that we should not "meet."

After the initial entrance (campaign),
every other vowe' in "politician"—is "I,"
until the end (re-campaign).

"A politician thinks of the next election;
a statesman—of the next generation."
—James Freeman Clarke

Politicians who remark,
"let history (prove) my decisions,"
do not strategize for the future—
but the past, ever.

Greed—is a separation from "agreed."

To adjust—is to accept circumstance.
To adapt—overcomes circumstance,
devising solution towards vision.

[To believe there's a need for Internet laws
(theft—is theft)
or law upon law, defining noun.]

Law directs action of man's mind—
not the tool of choice.

When men are no longer seen as men—
but adjectives—
men kill.

The only support of war:
support of ties—to the self.

If freedom can only be gained by death—
then laws—
are meaningless.

Do not worry about how much
you write in a day.
That is the heinous side of writing.

If one wishes to write poignantly,
write effortlessly (bit by bit).
Do not force.

What Cheek:

(Pronunciation is more important than spelling;
as man communed for centuries without a written form.)

Cheek is "chi" + "ka."
Chi, "intrinsic energy."
Intrinsic: "belonging to its very nature."
Energy: "...the ability to act, lead others, effect
things forcefully."
Ka, Egyptian, "soul."

Hence, any problems with "cheek," mean "that the
people around one—cannot handle the innate force
that one is; and one has obligingly sought to sequester
that God fire to a lesser portion, so as not to be
reprimanded by lesser souls—over acts which lead, and
direct others.

People with "chi-ka" were meant to lead. Let it out.
The world needs correcting. Politeness has caused
millenniums to pass without growth.

Awareness—is limited to
circumference of acquaintance.

Man does not pay attention to man,
until an introduction has been made.

Family—
is a byproduct
of one's emotions.

When one buys land at a parceled price,
and sells it at a profit—
one takes food from the next generation,
and starves the generations there after.

Humans keep their sensitivity—
by living in open spaces
(many acres).
(Don't believe me? I cite the city, and its laws.)

To state, "do not believe,"
implies
credibility—to its existence.

To spend time spying—
eradicates time achieving.
Centuries evaporate.

Those who initiate war, state:
"This—is the only way
one could stop me—
from harming others."

That armies still exist—
proves the human race
hasn't evolved initellectually.

We live in stone and wood;
and by altered names,
convince ourselves—
it is something very different,
from what it is.

If a word is governed by an adjective,
change the name of the "objective"—
alter the course upon which humans grow.

One cannot argue the future—by history.
History wasn't us; wasn't you.
To begin its argument—
believes in restitution by reincarnation.

Slander—argues the person, not the point.
Philosophy—argues the point, not the person.

The world is made in drops.

How do we teach to dream
if all imagined plot—
is conflict and ego.

Arguments beginning, "I think," or "I believe"—
are reflective of perception,
not what actually is.

When one sees, but does not listen,
one will not understand, what one sees.

That men write, "with love," on bombs,

proves—

that men do no know what love is.

For military personnel

to defend U.S. law outside the country,

yet—break U.S. law inside its borders—on leave,

said individual does not believe in the U.S.,

or the rights of its citizens,

but merely a paycheck.

If growth's metaphor is ascension,
then leaders who fear heights—
will oppose the dreams of the world.

Presidents (and ex-Presidents)
never have to live next to
the military they create.

The word "<u>congress</u>"—is not "<u>progress</u>."

Outrage against the governing laws—
is the epitome of the First Amendment.

"We have nothing to fear—
but fear, itself."

—Franklin Roosevelt.

America—
is the promise of all its presidents;
not just one.

When pain—becomes far greater than fear—
those—will stop at nothing—
to gnaw their own limbs
from the trap created.

This—
is why war—is ineffective.

It does not uphold "...*Life, Liberty,
and the Pursuit of Happiness...*"

If one desires the right to live around others—
then one must respect the rights of others
that one lives around.

Difference in opinion—
does not destroy
the value of the whole.

To cite the body,
leads not spiritually.

The calm voice—is the strongest.
Strength—does not mean truth.
Truth—is not associated with emotion.
Calm—is an emotion.

All sides are true.
The whole requires all sides.

To say, "on my side,"
risks one's growth.

"...will remove the candlestick out of his <u>place</u>,
except thou repent." —Rev. 2:5

Rod Parsley: *"Place, in Greek, is "topos."* (TBN 3/03)

The meaning of "topos":

Egyptians did not pronounce the letter "t";
it was a mark signifying end.
The word "op" means "eye."
The word "os" means "tooth."

"The eye of the tooth" means:
the vision of speech;
the wisdom of one's words.

"will remove the light (brilliance)
out of the wisdom of your words,
unless you repent."

Divide men—
they will creep success
by the century.

The future exists—
not by endangering the self,
but by risking the self.

Risk—does not harm anyone—
except one's self.

(Why war cannot solve world's problems.)

"Kill them all. Let God sort them out."

Assumes God—
rewards murder.
Does God not have the power to take?
(Need or require man to perform that act?)

Life—is time for self-solution.

If there wasn't free will—
how would one answer
the test of character—of the soul.

A question of God.
To perform the action—
is to become the action.

Assumption—is the worst profit.
It opens the door—for opportunity.

In the sunlit winter woods,
can only see the raven—
as a shadow on the ground.

((Unto the denunciation of wisdom):

God gave man a brain—
not a remote control.

All things are round.
Limbs; roots; fingers; eyes.
Yet—man builds, paints, and maps—in squares.

Slanted journalism—instigates.

A moneyless society is possible—
when there are no longer men
who need to be superior by possession.

Hence:
Land is taxed;
All men are slaves;
Freedom—is a paper pass (money);
Emptiness—is the slave master.

When 1/3 of a man's salary is taken as taxes—
he is but an indentured servant,
not a free man.

Mount Olympus, "up above the clouds,"
is "to always see the sun,"
or, "attainment, by optimism."

Mourning dove took flight
at tomato-dipped saltine,
viewed through a crack
between the window sill, and sheer.

Insanity—is the inability—to prove intuition.

Crazy—is a common term—
to conceal one's own stupidity.

Weird—is peer-pressure slang,
slandering creativity.

Some study psychology—
to learn how to manipulate.

Patience, lack of ego, and genuine care—
are the determiners.
These—can only be faked—for so long.

Fear—is the excuse of man.
One must eradicate fear in one's self—
before one can eradicate fear—in others.

Men will promote—what they are.

Men who don't like to include women—
in <u>all</u> things—
do not like women.

It is easy to feed the raven.
It is difficult to get the raven—
to eat from your hand.

"The problem is—that people don't think."

Thinking—is not the problem.
It is the thoughts—
one possesses,
with which to think.

A mere slender sapling branch,
can conceal a star;
yet—twigs, trees—move with earth.
Growth: studies movement.

(Fallacy of *the Bible* as The Guide.)

No one has ever acquired wisdom,
by reading one book.

If dreams have no meaning—
neither does life.

Men fear what lore is passed down,
because they do not seek to question its truth.
The mental work involved—requires much time;
and time, for most, is spent on luxuries of bodies.

Man—is an animal—
when he does not ascribe to
"I think, therefore, I am."

The power of the story—can dispel.

A man who owns his mind—
is richest of all.

If it is an animal
one wishes to sacrifice.
Sacrifice the animal—within.

The corrupt—can never see innocence.

Why do men accept surgery on the inside,
but not on the outside.
Surgery inside: "dead men walking."

Civil Liberty v. Civil Rights

A liberty—
is an infringement
on a right.

("Unpatriotic; hypocrisy; heresy; lunacy; etc.")

The closer one gets to truth,
the more the "in-power" crowd
slanders the examination.

Those who "photo-op"
have no power.
Their power—rests in what others think of them.

If man told the seed how to grow—
would it grow as effortlessly?

(Typo on warrant, etc.)

Intention—of application—
must be considered in law.
Else, intention it upholds, is criminal negligence.

It is not "...one nation, indivisible, under God..."
but, "...one nation, under God, indivisible..."

The Eisenhower Administration believed
in one world dominance of religion.

The inference: God—is indivisible,
not the nation.

It is indignant
for one to dump one's own problems
on others' doorsteps.

One with honor and self-ability
(what is mistakenly called "a man," "an adult")
tends to one's own problems.

Intellect—does not make one compassionate.
Compassion—is eroded by ambition.

Without honesty—
one denies others
the test of their soul.

Those who are offended at "forthrightness,"
prefer slander—in the off hours:
(When one is not around to defend one's self).

Excerpts from
Gnomon (philosophical verse)
by Ann Marie Yeager

~

Masters' Lesson IX {9}

Suicide is the yardstick,
'gainst which collectively measure,
our reflected inner worth.

~

...the soul is seated in the brain,
for all neural network relays back to it.

~

Churches like to preach,
let in the light of God,
by windows, either stained, or very small;
thus, their words are spoken in 90% darkness.

~

Only when presented with choice of two ideal candidates,
may one presume, there is no obligation to vote.

~

This be true,
we ne'er do,
hate a person.

We learn to hate
the ingrate,
of assertion.

~

An embrace in love—it doth endure,
and knows no time, or space, or cure.